BEWARE!
KILLER PLANTS

DESTRUCTIVE PLANTS

by Joyce Markovics

CHERRY LAKE PRESS
Ann Arbor, Michigan

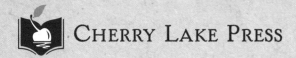

CHERRY LAKE PRESS

Published in the United States of America by Cherry Lake Publishing Group
Ann Arbor, Michigan
www.cherrylakepublishing.com

Reading Adviser: Beth Walker Gambro, MS Ed., Reading Consultant, Yorkville, IL
Content Adviser: Angie Andrade, Senior Horticulturist, Denver Botanic Gardens
Book Designer: Ed Morgan

Photo Credits: © RustyKitty/Shutterstock, cover and title page; © Reality Images/Shutterstock, 4; © EVGEIIA/Shutterstock, 5; © Sarah2/Shutterstock, 6; Michael Becker, Wikimedia Commons, 7; © Justin Runyon, 8; © Justin Runyon, 9 top; © freepik.com, 9 bottom; © IrinaK/Shutterstock, 10; © KAVIN PHONGSATANAKORN/Shutterstock, 10 background; © IrinaK/Shutterstock, 10 inset; © IrinaK/Shutterstock, 11; © Sukanin 18/Shutterstock, 12–13; George Jumara, U.S. Army Corp of Engineers, Wikimedia Commons, 13; © korkiatt/Shutterstock, 14; © wasanajai/Shutterstock, 15; © Rob Hainer/Shutterstock, 16; © Stock for You/Shutterstock, 17; © North Wind Picture Archives/Alamy Stock Photo, 18; Public Domain, 19 top; © F_studio/Shutterstock, 19 bottom; © issara sanguansak/Shutterstock, 20; © Wako Megumi/Shutterstock, 21 top; © SIMON SHIM/Shutterstock, 21 bottom; Wikimedia Commons, 22.

Copyright © 2022 by Cherry Lake Publishing Group
All rights reserved. No part of this book may be reproduced or utilized in any form or by any means without written permission from the publisher.

Cherry Lake Press is an imprint of Cherry Lake Publishing Group.

Library of Congress Cataloging-in-Publication Data

Names: Markovics, Joyce L., author.
Title: Destructive plants / by Joyce Markovics.
Description: Ann Arbor, Michigan : Cherry Lake Publishing, [2021] | Series:
   Beware! killer plants | Includes bibliographical references and index. |
   Audience: Grades 4-6
Identifiers: LCCN 2021001252 (print) | LCCN 2021001253 (ebook) | ISBN
   9781534187672 (hardcover) | ISBN 9781534189072 (paperback) | ISBN
   9781534190474 (pdf) | ISBN 9781534191877 (ebook)
Subjects: LCSH: Poisonous plants—Juvenile literature. | Dangerous
   plants—Juvenile literature.
Classification: LCC QK100.A1 M375 2021 (print) | LCC QK100.A1 (ebook) |
   DDC 581.6/59—dc23
LC record available at https://lccn.loc.gov/2021001252
LC ebook record available at https://lccn.loc.gov/2021001253

Printed in the United States of America
Corporate Graphics

CONTENTS

Dodgy Dodders

A neon-colored, spaghetti-like mass covers a large tree. It looks like an alien life-form. But the mass is actually a plant parasite called cuscuta. Its common name is dodder. This strange plant doesn't have roots or leaves. Instead, it has many slender stems.

Dodder draped over a tree

Dodder stems grow out of the soil. Then they seek out nearby plants, such as trees. Once they find a good host, they wind themselves around it like string.

A dodder grows on a potato bush.

Dodder is also called strangle weed or witches' shoelaces.

Then the dodder attacks! The stems have tiny parts called haustoria that can pierce tree bark. The haustoria suck out the tree's nutrient-filled sap. Over time, the tree dies—and the dodder survives.

Dodder is found throughout North America and Europe. This red dodder is growing in the United Kingdom.

A dodder's flower

Dodder plants can't make their own food. That's why they grow on and attack host plants. "It's probably one of the creepiest plants I know," says plant scientist Colin Purrington. "It's a horrible existence for the host plant."

Dodders can come in a rainbow of bright colors—except green. Dodder plants don't have chlorophyll. Chlorophyll is the green substance that helps plants make energy using light from the sun.

A young dodder only has a few days to find a host plant before it dies. How does it do this? Experts say it "smells" its host almost like an animal does. Dodder plants can pick up chemicals in the air. The chemicals signal to the dodder that a tasty plant is nearby.

A young dodder grows toward a tomato plant—one of its favorite hosts.

Dodders are one of many destructive plants around the world. Besides killing other plants, this group of plants can clog waterways, destroy property, and even poison the soil!

Once the dodder finds the tomato plant, it wraps around the stem of the plant.

Studies show that dodder plants prefer certain plants over others. They especially love juicy tomato plants.

Wicked Water Plants

Some lakes and swamps in the southern United States are being swallowed by a monster plant. It's called giant salvinia. Millions of these aquatic ferns float on the water's surface. They look like a thick green blanket.

Giant salvinias have air-filled leaves and feathery roots that allow them to float.

A mat of salvinias can grow up to 3 feet (1 meter) thick. One of the largest mats covered 96 square miles (249 square kilometers)!

Even more troubling, salvinias can double their numbers every 2 days. Over time, they can take over entire waterways. Boating and swimming can become nearly impossible. Salvinias also crowd out the **native** animals and plants living in the water.

Water hyacinth

Like salvinia, water hyacinth is a floating aquatic weed with feathery roots. Despite its pretty flowers, it chokes waterways and steals nutrients from the water.

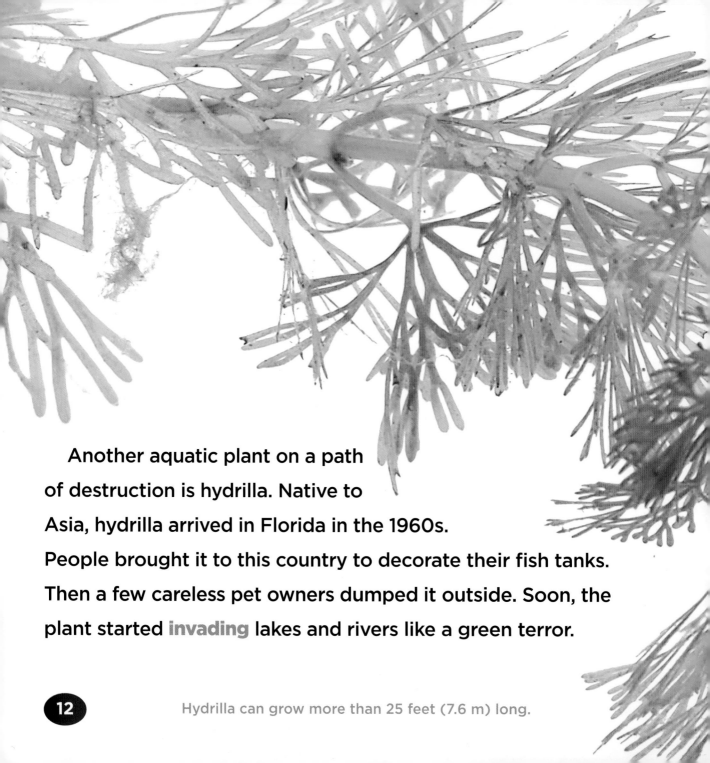

Another aquatic plant on a path of destruction is hydrilla. Native to Asia, hydrilla arrived in Florida in the 1960s. People brought it to this country to decorate their fish tanks. Then a few careless pet owners dumped it outside. Soon, the plant started **invading** lakes and rivers like a green terror.

Hydrilla can grow more than 25 feet (7.6 m) long.

Hydrilla is a prolific plant with strong roots. It can grow up to 1 inch (2.5 centimeters) each day. Hydrillas form a dense mat at the water's surface. They block out sunlight, and the water stagnates. The foul water creates a perfect home for disease-spreading mosquitoes.

Experts say it's almost impossible to get rid of hydrilla. Even the tiniest piece of a hydrilla can regrow into a new plant.

Hydrilla is a double threat. It also hosts a blue-green algae that can be deadly to some birds. Other types of algae can kill fish.

CREEPING KILLER

The destructive purple nutsedge plant kills as it creeps. Many experts call it the "world's worst weed." This fast-growing plant lives all over the world. It's often found in fields used for growing crops.

Purple nutsedge is also called coco-grass.

The tubers of the purple nutsedge

When farmers work the soil, they make the problem worse by breaking up the plant's **tubers**. Each tuber grows into a new plant. That's when disaster strikes. The tubers can release substances that poison the soil and kill plants growing nearby.

In some areas of Australia, the purple nutsedge has reduced the sugarcane harvest by as much as 75 percent.

Kudzu on the Loose

In the southern United States, everyone knows kudzu by name. Why? This destructive plant can pull down power lines. It can even cover an entire house. The kudzu vine moves like an army of snakes. It slithers across the ground and up and over trees and buildings.

Kudzu is known as "the plant that ate the South."

During summer, kudzu can grow 1 foot (0.3 m) per day. As it grows, kudzu sends out dozens of stems and puts down new roots. One kudzu root can weigh 400 pounds (181 kilograms). In a matter of weeks, the vine can engulf a small town.

People sometimes call kudzu "mile-a-minute" vine.

Americans were introduced to kudzu, which is native to Asia, in 1876. The fast-growing vine has big leaves and purple, grape-scented flowers. Gardeners and farmers alike loved it. By the 1900s, they had planted millions of vines.

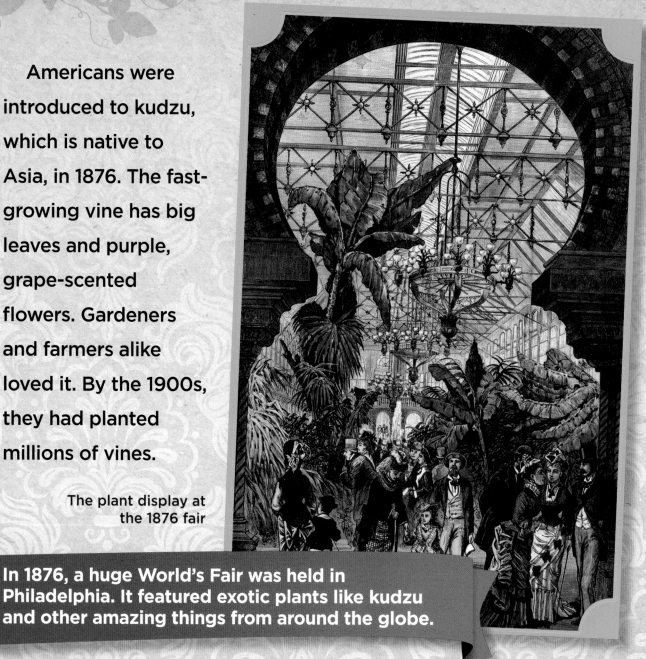

The plant display at the 1876 fair

In 1876, a huge World's Fair was held in Philadelphia. It featured exotic plants like kudzu and other amazing things from around the globe.

Farmers fed kudzu to their animals. And they planted it to stop erosion. The government also hired workers to plant kudzu along roadways. Soon, the vine was growing all over the South.

Cows and other farm animals feasted on kudzu.

As kudzu spread over thousands of acres, southerners tried to get rid of it. They poisoned, cut, and burned it. People also used animals to control the weed. Goats and sheep happily gobbled up the vines.

A sweet kudzu-flavored dessert

As it turns out, kudzu is quite tasty. People enjoy eating it too! They boil or fry the leaves as a snack. Sometimes, people use the flowers to make a sweet purple jelly or dessert.

Kudzu vines are home to an insect pest, the kudzu bug. This small beetle can cause a burning feeling on a person's skin.

A kudzu bug

PLANT PARTNERS

Plants and animals sometimes help one another.
This type of relationship is called mutualism.

Honeybees often visit kudzu flowers to get nectar and pollen to eat. In return, the honeybees pollinate the plant. They fly from flower to flower, spreading pollen and helping kudzu reproduce.

Kudzu

Kudzu produces purple flowers that smell like grapes. Bees harvest the flowers' pollen and nectar and turn it into purple honey!

Honeybee

Honeybees pollinate the kudzu flowers, helping the plant reproduce and grow into news plants.

GLOSSARY

algae (AL-gee) a kind of nonflowering plant, such as seaweed, that lives in water

aquatic (uh-KWOT-ik) relating to water

engulf (en-GUHLF) to cover or swallow up someone or something

erosion (ih-ROH-zhuhn) the wearing away of soil by water or wind

existence (ig-ZI-stuhns) the state or fact of being alive

host (HOHST) a living thing on or in which another organism called a parasite grows

invading (in-VAYD-ing) trying to take over an area

native (NAY-tiv) living or growing naturally in a place

nectar (NEK-tur) a sweet liquid produced by plants

nutrient (NOO-tree-uhnt) a substance needed by plants to grow and stay healthy

parasite (PA-ruh-site) a living thing that gets food by living on or in another living thing

pollen (POL-uhn) tiny yellow grains that are part of a plant's process of reproduction

prolific (pruh-LIF-ik) producing something in large quantities

stagnates (STAG-nayts) to become stale or foul, such as water

tubers (TOO-buhrz) the thick underground stems of certain plants

Find Out More

Books

Hirsch, Rebecca E. *When Plants Attack: Strange and Terrifying Plants*. Minneapolis: Millbrook Press, 2019.

Lawler, Janet. *Scary Plants*. New York: Penguin Young Readers, 2017.

Thorogood, Chris. *Perfectly Peculiar Plants*. Lake Forest, CA: Words & Pictures, 2018.

Websites

National Geographic Kids: Green Invaders
https://kids.nationalgeographic.com/explore/science/green-invaders/

Spot on Science: Invasive Plants
https://www.ideastream.org/programs/newsdepth/spot-on-science-invasive-plants

USDA Cooperative Extension: Invasive Species
https://invasive-species.extension.org/kids-page/

Index

About The Author

Joyce Markovics enjoys writing about and collecting unusual plants. One of her favorites is a huge, striped sansevieria with leaves that look like eels. She'd also like to add a whale fin sansevieria to her indoor garden.